Once Upon a Prayer

How to Hear God in Your Heart

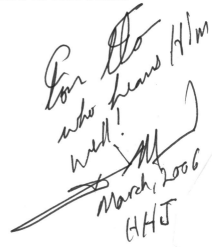

For Flo
who hears Him
well!

March, 2006

HHJ

About this book. . . .

It is meant for those to whom God is a reality—a personal, caring Creator. It is for those who believe that He put them on earth for a reason—to become His companions for time and eternity.

It has been suggested that the book and the writer's exercise it contains should be only for those who have read at least the New Testament and are in the process of reading the entire Bible.

I would concur. When someone discovers the reality of God, they are overwhelmed by the depths of His love for them. They want to devour the record of that love. If they could, they would read the Bible in one sitting because they now know it is His inspired Word. Anyone who does not feel that way, should not attempt this book.

But if you do feel that way, even if it's been years since you first experienced His love, this book *is* for you.

Jesus said: "My sheep hear my voice" (John 10:27). Taking Him at His word, this book will encourage the reader to begin to converse with Him—and regain his first love of Him.

Recently an old friend was in despair, going through a dark night of the soul. I gave him the manuscript of this book. When he came to Chapter 11 and did the writer's exercise—he connected. The first thing he heard the Father say was, *If you were the only person on earth, I would still have sent My Son for you.*

My sheep hear my voice,
and I know them,
and they follow me.

Also by the author...

The Last Awakening
Bosnia: Hope in the Ashes
Medjugorje Under Siege
The Gathering
Like a Mighty River
The Jesus Factor

History

(coauthored with Peter Marshall)
Sounding Forth the Trumpet
From Sea to Shining Sea
The Light and the Glory

Fiction

A Matter of Principle
A Matter of Time
A Matter of Diamonds
A Matter of Roses
Hellbound

Once Upon a Prayer

How to Hear God in Your Heart

David Manuel

Foreword by John Sherrill

McDougal Publishing is a ministry of The McDougal Foundation, Inc., a Maryland nonprofit corporation dedicated to spreading the Gospel of the Lord Jesus Christ to as many people as possible in the shortest time possible.

Published by:
McDougal Publishing
P.O. Box 3595
Hagerstown, MD 21742-3595
www.mcdougalpublishing.com

ISBN 1-58158-085-1

Printed in the United States of America

For Worldwide Distribution

Acknowledgments

When a writer looks up from the manuscript page, what he sees often influences what goes on that page. The writer of this book was blessed with two ocean views—first of the Atlantic, then of the Pacific—which conveyed both the magnitude of God's power and the depth of His love.

Benedict urged those who looked to him for spiritual leadership, to treat each guest as if he were Jesus Himself. During this book project, the author was the twice-blessed recipient of Benedictine-style hospitality. For the first half, he was a guest at the Atlantic Beach house of Charlie and Katy Towers. No other beach (with the possible exception of our own Nauset) is as conducive to the gathering of gossamer—the first phase of any book project.

For the second half, he was a guest at Villa Serena. This intimate, tucked-away inn on the Pacific coast of

Costa Rica is an extension of John Murphy's legendary Land Ho in Orleans on Cape Cod. From its open but roofed upper deck, the view of the surf was unchanging and eternal—like the One about whom the author was attempting to write.

December 2004

Contents

Foreword

[From John Sherrill's *Guideposts* article "Pencil in Hand"]

A surprising—and surprisingly effective—way to pray...

I'd never known our friend David Manuel to be so emphatic. My wife, Tib, and I had climbed up to his lighthouse studio overlooking Cape Cod Bay. But David, we quickly learned, hadn't invited us up there for the view.

"I want to show you something new," he said, handing each of us a pencil and a legal-sized yellow pad. "A new way to pray. Imagine yourself climbing the Mount of Olives. You come to a clearing—and there is Jesus, alone, seated on a bench. He motions you to join Him, invites you to talk to Him about anything that's on your mind or in your heart. Write down what you say to Him. Listen to His response. Record the whole conversation on your yellow pad."

We were journalists, Tib and I. We've interviewed hundreds if not thousands of people. But this was the most unusual conversation either of us had ever been asked to record.

For an hour we experimented with this technique so unlike our usual inside-our-heads prayer approach. Back home next morning, I got up early, took coffee, pencil, and pad out to our porch and, as David instructed, imagined Jesus sitting there.

Away from David's lighthouse, however, doubts and questions assailed me. What tone was appropriate? Formal and worshipful, or casual and everyday? Finally I just plunged ahead. "Well, Lord, here I am," I wrote on the first ruled line. "If You want to know what is *really* on my mind, I'm worrying about our old car breaking down on our trip south."

I waited, then wrote down what I thought I heard.

That worry is masking a bigger concern. Your own aging. Your own health breaking down.

What? I was feeling great! Well, a few aches and pains maybe, but I wasn't the kind of guy who went running to the doctor with every little complaint. "All right, Father," I wrote, "You must be right. I'm almost eighty-two, and I'm afraid I won't be able to keep up our travel schedule indefinitely."

Back and forth the dialogue went—other subjects, other insights, corrections, encouragements. Was I really hearing from God? Or were these just my own thoughts? In David's lighthouse, I'd jotted down two of his yardsticks for measuring anything I heard: Were the responses in keeping with the personality of Jesus? And were they consistent with Scripture? Against these standards, I found this first dialogue acceptable. If it was something important and I had doubts, David also advised, I should check with a trusted and experienced Christian friend.

I put my yellow pad aside, astonished to find that forty minutes had sped by! I returned to my porch rendezvous every morning for a month. Then Tib and I set out on that editorial trip through the South. It was our second week on the road, a Thursday in Louisiana, when one of my upper left molars began to throb. Root canal trouble, I thought. When next day the pain spread to the lower jaw, I phoned my endodontist back in New York. "He says it doesn't sound like a tooth problem," I reported to Tib. By bedtime I was wincing with an earache too.

All night I tossed on that motel bed. The whole left half of my face was on fire. By the next morning it was •

spotted with red lesions the size of nickels. A little boy saw me in the breakfast room and ran screaming to his mother.

Tib had been on the phone trying to locate a doctor. Naturally, it was a Saturday (when else do health crises occur?). I put on dark glasses, pulled my hat down to cover as much of my face as possible, and let Tib drive me some thirty miles to the nearest hospital emergency room. We waited for three hours until the frazzled young physician on duty could see me.

He did a quick examination, took some cultures, and informed me that I had a bacterium. "This should clear it up," he said, writing out a prescription for an antibiotic. "Stop and see another doctor if it doesn't get better."

It didn't. Monday we reached Lindale, Texas, where Tib had a teaching commitment. Lindale was just big enough to support a one-physician clinic. We made an appointment with Dr. Anthony Davis.

He listened to my report of the emergency room physician's diagnosis. Then he looked up from his note-taking. "This is a textbook case of shingles," he said firmly. I didn't much like the diagnosis. But I liked the confidence in his voice.

Dr. Davis had recognized my problem the minute I walked through the door. The telltale sign was lesions on just one side of the face. "I don't see how any…" He stopped himself, but the rest of the sentence hung in the air—how could an even marginally trained doctor have missed something so obvious? "Shingles is a virus, not a bacterium; antibiotics don't help," he went on. Apparently the disease can appear in anyone who's had chickenpox. The virus lies dormant in the body—in my case for more than seventy years—until some agent reactivates it. "Have you been under stress lately?" the doctor asked.

Of course I'm under stress, I thought. *Who isn't?* There was the stress of traveling, and worrying about our kids and grandkids, and okay, maybe worrying about my health. If stress could trigger shingles, I didn't see how anyone could escape.

"Unfortunately," Dr. Davis resumed, "you've missed the critical window of time." If shingles is treated within seventy-two hours, he said, you could usually prevent the serious pain which so often persists long after the initial attack.

Dr. Davis gave me a prescription, "just in case we're not too late." As I left, he added the advice doctors are so fond of giving: "Avoid stress."

How was I supposed to do that?

The trip stretched on and so did the pain. The tension made me grind my teeth even in the daytime. I was miserable, and miserable to be with, no doubt. Surly. Snappish. Impatient. As I caught myself with a tight-clenched jaw, I seemed to hear, *Have you forgotten our morning conversations?*

I'd kept at my prayer-with-a-pencil each morning before we left. But on the road it hadn't happened. We'd been too busy, I thought. Now the horrible pain demanded an action. Sitting in the lobby of a motel in Arkansas the next day, I drew out my pencil and yellow pad.

You're angry, I heard.

"Angry, Lord?" I wrote. "At whom?"

At the doctor who didn't spot shingles.

I knew at once that this was truth, though I hadn't wanted to admit it. "How can I help it? I deserve to be angry."

Write a letter.

My pencil wrote furiously. To whom should I write? The director of the hospital? Threaten them with a malpractice suit? These things would certainly discharge my anger, but… were they consistent with the personality of Jesus? Somehow I could not imagine Him initiating a legal battle. Nor damaging a man's reputation with his employer. However, I could envisage Jesus addressing a poorly performing individual directly.

Well, honestly and firmly, but with understanding.

When we got home, I wrote the ER doctor. So far I have not heard back. If the doctor fails to reply, I will dialogue again with Jesus, asking Him what to do. Meanwhile, I've stopped grinding my teeth. Maybe all I needed to do was *write* that letter.

I've seen six doctors since the onset of shingles, including the head of the pain management clinic at New York Presbyterian. I've lived on Motrin and Neurontin and a cornucopia of other medications. Four months into this ordeal, the discomfort is finally diminishing, though I still frighten callers at the front door with the Lidoderm patches I wear for twelve hours a day in strips across the nerve paths on my face.

Do I still dialogue in the early morning? Yes, indeed. I pray with my pencil. My sessions extend beyond strictly personal matters—pain and anger have a way of dominating the horizon—to include daily thanksgivings and intercessions, and pleas for simple guidance. And never before in my life have I felt so close to God in prayer.

The doctors' best guess is that it will take another three months before I'm pain free. So I'm on the mend, which is good news. The better news is the new way Tib and I discovered to pray. With pencil in hand.

John Sherrill
Roving Editor, *Guideposts*

To
the memory of
Hal Helms,
who was listening
long before I was

1

The Voice

In the spring of 1995, I came within a millimeter of dying. That, as the postop biopsy revealed, was how close the cancer had come to escaping from my right kidney. Had it gotten out, it would have spread everywhere, and I would have died of stomach cancer—exactly as my father had, six years before.

The first morning home after the operation, I was dozing in the April sun that streamed in through the bedroom window. I was in no pain; the Percocet was taking care of that. But it had also constricted my urinary tract, to the point where I'd had to have a catheter reinserted.

Now, as I lay there half awake and steeped in self-pity, I heard a voice in the depths of my heart: *Get up. Come to your chair. I want to talk to you.*

I knew who it was. I'd heard that voice often in the

early days, once I'd discovered God was real, twenty-six years before. I'd been an editor at Doubleday then, the youngest in the biggest publishing house in the world. I was fast-tracking in the trade division, confident I was the brightest person I'd ever known.

Then God knocked me off my high horse. (I would later learn that this was known as a Damascus Road experience.) Before being unhorsed, I'd had no personal encounter with God.

My grandmother had. When I would go to her house for a weekend overnight, she insisted on reading Bible stories to me and made me go to her Presbyterian church's Sunday school. But she had terrible breath, and I counted the minutes till my parents would come for me.

We lived in Shaker Heights, where we went to Christ Episcopal Church. Eventually I served as an acolyte—though without any awareness of the reality of who we were worshiping.

Like most alumni of the boys' school I attended through the ninth grade, my favorite memory of Hawken was of the brief chapel service that opened and closed each day. Yet not even there was God real, though He must have been to the headmaster, Carl Holmes.

At Deerfield Academy, church was mandatory, as was Sunday Night Sing, where we sang hymns and listened to inspiring (albeit nonevangelical) talks by visiting speakers. Neither there nor afterwards at Yale was the reality of God ever addressed. That, of course, did not keep me from formulating a strong opinion on the subject. I agreed with Nietzsche and his ilk: God was a hypothetical construct, imagined by an inferior people to comfort themselves. As Karl Marx put it, religion was the opiate of the proletariat.

At Naval Officer Candidate School I received an engraved Bible from the chaplain, but I never opened it. During four years in the Naval Air Force, flying radar patrols out of Newfoundland and Iceland, there were white-knuckle moments when I would have been grateful for Someone to pray to. But once I was back in civilian life, the need for a supernatural Protector quickly faded.

I was thirty-three years old, attending a lecture at Wainwright House in Rye, New York, on Palm Sunday, when I heard Him for the first time. The speaker was a scientist who had successfully demonstrated that plants (a rhododendron hooked up to the psychogalvanic skin response indicator of a polygraph) manifested a sub-emotional response to their environment. The effect had been replicated in good labs (Sloane-Kettering, McGill, UCLA Medical Center, Texas Instruments), and had been written up favorably in *Science*.

Plants responded to their environment? There really *were* green-thumbed people? I smelled a potential best-seller.

Now, the speaker confided, they had recently recorded, on a much muted level, a similar response from a piece of granite.

His audience gasped. With a wry smile he noted, "Science has no explanation for this."

As he spoke, the thought entered my heart: *That is because the explanation is too simple for science. The rock and the rhododendron have one thing in common: They were made by the same hand.*

I was stunned. Where did *that* come from?

Not from me. My intellect was appalled; it would *never* have made such a deduction!

Could it be from—God?

Was He—real?

In that instant, my world turned upside down. The scientist was still speaking as I got up and slipped out to find a place where I could be alone. In a library, standing beside a floor lamp next to a floor-to-ceiling wall of books, I tried to figure out what had just happened.

God? Was real?

My heart knew it was true, and my head wasn't even arguing.

Moreover, I felt—a presence. And also felt like I was bathed in invisible sunlight.

Another thought came, unbidden, into my heart, not my head: *You will never be alone again.*

My head *did* argue with that. I made friends easily—wherever I was, under whatever circumstances—and they were enduring friendships. At work, I never ate lunch alone. At home, my wife and I entertained frequently—in Princeton now, in Toronto before, where I'd set up an editorial department for Doubleday Canada. I probably had more good friends than anyone I knew.

And yet (as my heart reminded me when my head was finished), I was desperately lonely. I had no one to whom I could unburden myself. My wife Barbara had been that person, but communication, the thing that had drawn us together, had broken down several years before. Now there was no one.

No, said my heart. Now there was Someone.

Another heart thought came: *You need never be afraid again.*

To that, my head took vehement exception. I had sky-dived, taken a bronze medal in the downhill ski run at Mount Tremblant. There was nothing I was afraid of!

Then my heart reminded me that I was afraid of failure, afraid of the unknown, afraid of the future. Most of all, afraid of my father's disapproval. My earthly father, not...

You can stop despising yourself.

My head laughed at that. My air of superiority was legendary. My father's nickname for me whenever I returned home was "King of the Road." It was not a compliment.

My heart now pointed out that that was all a façade. In rare moments of candor, I knew I was a dilettante—a fake, callow, superficial person. My father was right.

But now—everything was different.

God was real.

And He cared.

As each heartthought came, it felt like another boulder had been removed from the invisible sack I'd been carrying. I felt lighter and lighter—until I was practically floating.

2

Mini Miracles

When I awoke the next morning, it was still there. *God was real.* My heart knew it. My head still had reservations, but I was beginning to distrust my intellect's conviction that it was always right. It had been wrong recently—gravely wrong.

For now, I would stick with my heart, and my heart said He was real. I felt like Dorothy after her house came down, opening the front door and discovering everything was in Technicolor!

Barbara and our three-year-old daughter, Blair, were down in Naples, Florida, visiting her parents. I was to fly down Friday, spend Easter with them, and bring them home. Meantime, rather than spend three hours a day commuting back and forth to an empty house in

Princeton, I was staying in the Upper West Side apartment of a friend who was out of town.

But now it was Monday, and I was scheduled to make a book proposal at the weekly editorial conference at Doubleday's head office on Park Avenue at 47th Street. The meeting was at 9:30, and it was 8:03—tight, but doable. I went out to the little Chinese laundry to get the dress shirt I would need. On my way, I noted that the colors seemed richer, almost saturated. And the mica chips in the sidewalk were like tiny diamonds.

At the laundry, I gave the Chinese woman behind the counter my ticket. She disappeared into the back room and returned in a moment, shirtless.

"Not there," she said tersely, trying to get me to take the ticket back.

That was my only clean shirt! "Please," I begged, fighting down panic, "look again. It's got to be there!"

"Not there!" she insisted, but she did return to the back.

I said my first prayer. "God, if You *are* real," I whispered, "I need that shirt."

How foolish, came the thought. ***You're praying to thin air.*** Maybe so, but desperate men do foolish things. The prayer stood.

In a moment she returned, scowling and shaking her

head. In her hands was a slim parcel wrapped in brown paper and tied with string. She thrust it at me. "Wasn't there!" she exclaimed in disgust.

There were goose bumps on my arms as I returned to my friend's apartment. I dressed quickly, but it was 8:55 by the time I was ready to leave. It was really tight now, but still doable.

Then I noticed it had begun to rain.

I hurried to the corner of 112th Street and Broadway, to hail a southbound cab. The trouble was, there were three other guys already at my intersection—all dressed like me in their Brooks Brothers raincoats and attaché cases, their tightly furled umbrellas now open. They were all trying to get a cab. And up Broadway at the intersection above us, others were doing the same.

There were plenty of southbound cabs hurtling over the hill, but not one had its "available" light on.

I glanced at my watch: 9:10. Too late to make a dash for the subway. Almost too late for a cab, if by some miracle I was able to get one.

Miracle? I said my second prayer.

Nothing happened.

See? Thin air.

Dejected, I left the corner and wandered up Broadway towards the subway station. I was going to be at least half an hour late, probably more. But I let the prayer stand.

And then one of the unlit cabs pulled over right in front of me. The door opened, an old lady paid her fare and got out, and I got in—this time with more than goose bumps. My scalp tightened, and frost crept up my backbone.

I made it to the editorial conference room just in time to join the others going in. They liked my proposal, and as the meeting broke up I murmured to my good friend Alex Liepa, "Can you get free for lunch? It's important."

As our religion editor, Alex worked closely with Billy Graham, Oral Roberts, and Kathryn Kuhlman. If anyone could tell me what was happening to me, he could.

But over lunch, as I described the shirt incident and then the cab incident, he grew increasingly agitated. "And so," I concluded, "either I'm going insane, or—God is hand-tailoring mini miracles in response to specific requests."

Alex put his fork down with a clatter. "Stop talking that way!" he hissed, looking around in hopes that no one had overheard me. "You're sounding like a Pentecostal or a Fundamentalist!"

I did not know what either of those words meant, but the way he said them, you didn't want to be them.

From that moment, I became a closet—whatever-I-was.

The next time I heard God was a couple of days later, in St. Bartholomew's Episcopal Church on Park Avenue. New at this prayer business, I figured it probably worked better in a church, and as St. Bart's was only four blocks up the street, it was easy enough to get to. Except—what exactly did you do?

Going down front, I slipped into a pew and gazed up at the Byzantine-style gold mosaic of Jesus on the Mount of Transfiguration. *God*, I thought, *I really want to get to know You better. I know You're real, but...* The thought trailed off. I didn't know what else to say.

Apparently that was enough. In my heart I heard, *The way to the Father is through the Son.*

That sounded like it came from the Bible, so when I got back to the office, I went to the editorial department's reference library. Sure enough, there was one there—a tattered old Douay Version. The tape holding on the cover had yellowed with age. Borrowing it overnight, I took it back to my friend's apartment.

It was not like I'd never read the Bible. We'd studied it in the eighth grade, as the earliest known example of epic literature. It had not made much of an impression.

Now, as I looked at the old Bible in my lap, I wondered where to begin. Well, if the way to the Father was through the Son, I should probably start with one of the gospels. I picked Luke.

I had not read more than a page, when I froze—what I held in my hands was not literature; it was history.

I devoured Luke and then John and then the book of Acts—and knew in my heart that every word was true.

One more instance of hearing God's voice in St. Bartholomew's occurred five months later. I had just come from my first TGIF gathering. On Fridays a group of Christian businessmen in Manhattan brought lunch to an unused IBM boardroom, to pray together and share what God had been doing in their lives.

Hearing of it, I screwed up my courage to the sticking point and went. And for the first time, I prayed and shared with other men. The last thing we did before going our separate ways was to join hands and say the

Lord's Prayer. I wished we weren't holding hands; I needed to wipe away the tears streaming down my face.

But as grateful as I was, I came away depressed. They were far more committed than I was. I talked the talk; they were walking the walk.

Before returning to my office, I slipped into St. Bart's. Not feeling particularly close to God, I entered a pew towards the back. Having been in the company of real Christians, I was convicted of how shallow and phony I was.

As I knelt there, I noticed something I'd felt a few times in the past couple of weeks, when I focused intently on God. There was the slightest movement of air around my face and the backs of my hands. I knew it was from Him, but I had no idea what it meant.

Then I heard in my heart: *I am calling you out to a life of service.*

As the words came, I saw in my mind a poster I'd seen that morning, riding in to work on the train. It was a picture of a bride and groom exchanging vows. And I realized why He was now recalling it to my memory. He was calling me to make a covenant with Him, equivalent to a marriage vow.

"If that's You," I whispered, "and if You're asking what I think You are, then—I accept."

That summer St. Bartholomew's was undergoing a major organ renovation, and often there would be a technician up in the organ loft. There was one up there now. On other days he had occasionally tried a note. But never had he done what he did now.

As I said, "I accept," the tech hit the biggest all-stops-out chord I had ever heard!

The organ roared! The church seemed to jump an inch off of Park Avenue! I bolted out of the pew and ran all the way back to the office.

I had accepted God's call—and at full volume, He had accepted my acceptance.

3

Dead Man Walking

That fateful Palm Sunday, 1970, when He revealed Himself to me, my world turned upside down. I gave up the fast track at Doubleday, joined a Christian community, and set up an editorial office for Logos, the first Charismatic publishing house.

In 1973, I began writing books for Him, and by 1995 I'd written or ghosted twenty-six, including a couple of best-sellers. I'd spoken around the country, had Christian friends around the world. I was walking the walk now, not just talking the talk.

But I was a dead man walking. There was no joy in my life—anywhere. I lived to ride my bicycle—to escape the surly bonds of my reality. I rode 120 miles a week, and in a ten-mile time trial managed to average 22.8 mph, making me the sixth fastest cyclist in my age-group in southeastern Massachusetts. It was an achievement of immense consequence to me, and utterly devoid of consequence to anyone else, including God.

The nadir came in early March. Barbara and I were in Naples, visiting her widowed mother for a week. I'd brought my bike, like golfers brought their clubs, and on our last day I'd ridden from Naples to Fort Myers and back. As I sat on the seawall contemplating this accomplishment, there was no sense of satisfaction, none of the exhilaration I'd expected. All I tasted was ashes.

Had my life devolved to this? What had happened to God? To my call to a lifetime of service? I realized that on my priority scale, He had fallen to around fourth or fifth (*actually, sixth*).

Not since I'd known Him, had my life felt so meaningless and empty.

Back home on the Cape, I flung myself into my obsessive fitness regime. It was too cold outside to ride, so I swam—every day, training hard the way I used to when I swam for Yale.

One day, as I was attempting to lower my best time for the mile, I heard a voice, harsh and mocking: *You're going to die soon!*

It so spooked me, I got out of the pool and went home. But the next day I was back again, pushing again, and this time there was no frightening surprise.

That came twelve hours later. Around two in the morning I got up to use the bathroom, as I normally did. But this time was far from normal. The urine in the toilet bowl was tinged with red, and there was a small, dark clot in it.

Blood.

I couldn't breathe. And was about to wake my wife, when I realized that all it would do was frighten her out of her wits, which would make two of us.

I could call our doctor, Bill Velie; he made house calls. Yet what could he do? Look in the bowl and say, "Yup, that's blood all right."

In the end, I waited until 7:30 AM when I knew he'd be in his office—the longest five hours of my life.

4

A Millimeter

Hearing the fear in my voice, Bill had me come to his office, where he spun a urine sample. To my immense relief, he informed me there wasn't anything out of the ordinary. In all probability I'd merely popped a blood vessel from the exertion of the mile time trial. Just to be on the safe side, however, he wanted me to go to the hospital in Hyannis to get an abdominal x-ray.

"But I feel fine now," I insisted. "Look, if it happens again, I'll certainly…"

Bill just smiled and nodded. "Go and get the x-ray."

The red-haired radiologist was cheerful, with a green shamrock on her white smock. It was Saint Patrick's Day, and she was from County Clare. She took the x-rays and disappeared.

When she returned to say that the doctor would like

to see some more, she was still smiling, so I didn't suspect anything. But when she came back and said that now he'd like to see an ultrasound, I frowned.

"What is it?"

"Sure now, you know I couldna' be tellin' you, even if I'd a mind to," said she, with a charming Irish lilt.

"Ah, not even a wee hint?" I bantered. "Just to put a poor heart at rest?"

"Not even that," she replied, with a grin. Cute. But very professional.

When she came back for another ultrasound, I laid it on the line. "For the love of Saint Patrick, will no one tell me what is transpiring in my nether regions?"

"Your doctor will be calling you."

After an eternity of waiting in the waiting room, I was paged to the phone. "They've found something," said Bill matter-of-factly.

"What?"

"I want you to talk to the urologist on duty."

"*Tell me!* "

"Talk to Dr. Billingsgate" (not his real name).

Very professional, I thought dourly, returning to the waiting room.

After another eternity, I was again paged. Dr. Billingsgate was between operations and could see me now.

I was shown into a consulting room adjacent to the operating room. The urologist appeared, a short. balding man in green scrubs with a manila envelope under his arm.

"Normally I'd tell you this in my office, with both of us sitting down, but," he nodded in the direction of the OR, "they'll be calling me, as soon as my next is anesthetized."

He put an x-ray up on a wall light table. "See this kidney?" He pointed to the left one—*my* left one. "It's normal. But this one," he tapped the other one, which was significantly larger and opaque, "is full of cancer. It's got to come out."

And with that, his beeper went off. "See my secretary," he said, heading for the OR. "She'll make the necessary appointments."

I stared after him, in shock. See his secretary? I couldn't move.

In a daze, I managed to find his office. Checking the schedule, his secretary informed me that they could get me in for a CAT scan in a week and a bone scan in ten days. After that, the doctor would meet with me and would schedule...

"Whoa! A week? Ten days? Isn't this an emergency?"

"Mr. Manuel," she declared, unable to keep the disdain out of her voice, "*all* of our cases are emergencies."

I drove home numb, wishing now that I'd brought someone with me. But it was supposed to be just a routine x-ray...

And then I remembered a forgotten detail of my father's losing battle with stomach cancer. The first indication he'd had that anything was wrong, was when he had blood in his urine. Eight months later he was gone.

Eight months... Would Barbara be able to keep the house? I'd have to go over the finances with her, work out a budget. The royalties were adequate, but they were diminishing. She might have to take a job.

When I got home, Bill Velie was waiting with Barbara. Seeing my expression, he said, "I think we should take one step back from the graveside. You're going to lose a kidney, not your life. In fact," he chuckled, "your life really isn't going to change that much."

For the next three days we were inundated with so much good advice about hospitals and surgeons that our receptors burned out. (I say "we," because, as anyone whose spouse has gone through a life-threatening illness knows, the two become one—and the ordeal is harder on the one married to the patient.)

Finally, in desperation, we prayed, "Father, just get us to the right surgeon in the right hospital at the right time. We put it in Your hands."

Three days later we were in the office of Dr. Alex Althausen, Massachusetts General Hospital's ace surgeon for kidneys and prostates. He was a living legend, and deservedly so.

In three more days I went under the knife—smiling.

As we climbed the front steps of Mass General, there was so much undergirding prayer that I actually tried to entertain a negative thought. I looked up; would it be the last time I ever saw the sky?

I just grinned. That was the power and depth of the intercessory prayer covering me! All our friends at home were praying, plus we'd sent an urgent prayer request to friends around the world. I felt like I was riding a surfboard on a breaking wave of grace!

Never again would I be less than wholeheartedly committed when someone asked me to pray for them.

The admitting nurse said, "You know, you're lucky they caught this. We call kidney cancer the hidden killer. By the time someone knows something's wrong, it's usually too late to save them."

The operation took five hours. A biopsy of the removed kidney revealed that the cancer had come within a millimeter of escaping. In another week or ten days…

5

Hearing His Voice

et up. Come to your chair. I want to talk to you. He had to say it three times before I grumpily got out of bed and gingerly carried my catheter bag over to my easy chair. On the way, I picked up my clipboard with its ever-present yellow legal pad, in case He might say something worth writing down.

You know I have extended your life for a purpose.

Yes.

Do you know what it is?

I guess the first thing is to rearrange my priorities. Put You first.

What else?

Get serious about serving You.

What else?

Be more thoughtful of those around me.

What else?

Consult with You before deciding anything.

What else?

It went on that way for about fifteen minutes. I sensed it could have gone on all morning, but I'd heard about all I could process.

Had it been anyone else saying such things to me, even the most gifted and appreciated counselor, after about the tenth or eleventh item, my heart might not have hardened, but my mind would have been wondering how soon the session was going to be over.

With Him it was different. He loved me—more than anyone ever had. Or would. Or could. And He had forgiven me, when, if I were Him, I would have washed my hands of me long ago. Instead, here He was, laying the foundation for a new life. It blew out all my circuits.

He *cared*. And because I knew to the depths of my being that He did, it made *me* care—and want to change. I had been arrogant, stuffed full of self and rebelling at even the thought of Him. Now all I wanted to do was draw closer to Him.

The next morning we had another talk. And the next morning, and the next. Each time, I would record what He said and what I said. My clipboard had become my spiritual journal.

It was difficult, at first, to hear Him consistently. The fault was mine, not His.

He spoke quietly—so quietly you might almost think you had imagined it. As Elijah discovered (1 Kings 19), His voice was still and small. To hear Him, one had to be completely at rest.

My mind was like an unruly child in church. I had not realized how difficult it was to suspend all thought, to shut out all distraction, to remain perfectly still, patiently abiding, like Elijah in the presence of the Lord.

I knew it was what He wanted—what He commanded: *"Be still, and know that I am God"* (Psalm 46:10). In my spirit, I sensed it was the way to that peace *"which passeth all understanding"* (Philippians 4:7). Did the Shepherd not lead His sheep beside the still waters? Did He not do it to restore their souls? (See Psalm 23:1-3.) My spirit was willing, but my soul had been having its own way for so long…

I chose peace, knowing that like other muscle groups, spiritual muscles grew stronger with use. Each morning, I would force myself to sit still, attentive, blackboard washed clean. And *no* multi-tasking. If it irritated me when someone with whom I was conversing was also doing something else, imagine how God must feel when we fail to give Him our undivided attention.

He was, I discovered, the soul of patience. He would give me a target word, like *love* or *jealousy* or *pride*, and would then elaborate on how it applied to my life. Sometimes I could hear Him easily, and could scarcely write fast enough to get down what He was saying. At other times, His response would come a phrase at a time, or even a word at a time.

Slowly I was getting the hang of it. The sheep *did* come to know the Shepherd's voice, but it took training. Sometimes, with one who was dumb or willful—or both (like me)—it took a great deal of training. But He had endless patience.

Some of the training was painful, as He showed me that the jealousy or ego or pride ran deeper than I thought. But even here, the love was omnipresent. As Paul reminded the Hebrews, what good father does not discipline his son, when it is called for? It is never pleasant at the time, but it produces a harvest of righteousness and peace for those who are trained by it. Conversely, anyone who manages to avoid discipline is illegitimate, not a true son. (See Hebrews 12:5-11.)

If I ever hit a dry patch, all I had to do was ask Him a question. He *always* answered questions—as I had answered my daughter when she was little and had an endless supply of questions. Part of what kept her asking was her need for assurance that I was there and paying attention.

He was there, and always would be, He assured His disciples, *"to the end of the age"* (Matthew 28:20).

All in all, it was a wondrous experience. Here I was, conversing with the Alpha and the Omega who had made heaven and earth! He and I, talking. Like He and Adam once had in the cool of the day. Like He and David did, as recorded in the Psalms. Like Elijah, learning to stand silent in His presence. Like Habakuk waiting on the rampart, ready to record whatever God would say to him. Like John on Patmos, writing down exactly what God showed him and told him.

Gradually I came to realize something. C. S. Lewis had said that the devil's greatest deception was to convince modern man that he did not exist. If that was so, then his second greatest was to convince modern believers that they could not hear the voice of their Creator in the depths of their hearts.

Dwelling on this one day as we dialogued, I recalled that in the beginning of my walk with Him, I used to talk with Him all the time; I thought everyone who knew Him did.

It was only later that I began to doubt my ability to hear Him. Like other new Charismatics, I became convinced that you couldn't actually *hear* Him.

Oh, in a life-and-death emergency, you might hear an audible voice say, "Do not get on that airplane!" But for the most part, we told one another, you got your guidance indirectly. You searched the Scriptures, asking God to quicken a verse to your spirit. The lazy man's version of this was known as Bible roulette or lucky dipping. You asked God a question, then opened the Bible at random and let your eye fall where it may. We all knew we shouldn't get our guidance this way—but we'd all done it, anyway.

Other methods were the open door/shut door prayer, the red light/green light prayer, or the make-me-anxious/make-me-peaceful prayer. And you could always cast a fleece. My favorite was suggested by an old friend: "All right, God, if You really want me to do this, let a Japanese admiral in full-dress uniform knock on my door between 9:00 and 9:03 tomorrow morning."

As a final check, you could always ask your Christian friends what they thought God's will was for you. I've never known any who were unwilling to give me the full benefit of their wisdom.

But now, as He began to show me different areas

where I needed to change, I began to suspect that the real reason I'd stopped dialoguing with Him in those early days was because I didn't care for what He was telling me.

Only now, I had been granted a life extension. I *had* to hear whatever He wanted to tell me—my life depended on it.

Each morning as I recovered from my operation, He and I would talk, after which I would type it up. After a month of these, my spiritual director confirmed that I was hearing the Holy Spirit. And encouraged me to periodically check what I was hearing with someone whose discernment I trusted, just to be sure I was not hearing some unholy spirit masquerading as Him.

Gradually I became aware that my listening-to-God times had become the most important part of my day—not always my favorite part, but the most important.

If I was running late and skipped it, the day would never go as well. And sometimes, when it started to go horribly, I would remember that I'd been too busy to stop and spend time with Him that morning.

Which brings us to the devil's third great deception

in the modern age: to fill our lives with such busyness that we do not have time for God. I used to think it was just me—but the more people I talked to, the more I became convinced that it's true of everyone. No one has enough time anymore. We can't get done during the day what must be done, so we take care of it after we get the kids to bed. No wonder we've grown so irritable and impatient as a society; America is running in a state of perpetual sleep deprivation.

Who has time to give God fifteen minutes, let alone more than that? The alarm clock goes off. We wash our faces, brush our teeth, and get back on the exercise wheel in the gerbil cage.

It's been said of one of the spiritual giants of an earlier age that he would give God the first two hours of his day. Except when he was under extreme, unrelenting pressure, with momentous pending consequences. Then he would give Him four.

Social psychologists tell us a habit takes twenty-one days to form, but only five to break. In my experience, prayer is one of the hardest habits to form, and the easiest to break. Especially the way I used to pray— which was almost all about me, and little, if any, about Him.

It was different now. There were two of us talking. And I never knew how He was going to respond. Real prayer, I came to realize, was a time of sharing—words and feelings and silence—an intimate time.

Yet even now I could get too busy. So I determined to give God the firstfruits of the day. (I tried giving Him the last fruits, but the moment I got quiet enough to hear Him, I fell asleep.)

And now I was finding that I needed Him more than just in the morning. There were too many crises, too many out-of-control situations. Like the old hymn said, I needed Him every hour.

I wasn't sure I liked that. All my life I'd been self-reliant—independent and proud of it.

Now I was growing dependent on Him.

6

Father and Son

It got to the point where I would fly to my journal in every predicament. I could hear Him off journal, but I didn't trust that method. I had a strong will and a strong ego; how could I be certain that one or both weren't informing what I seemed to be hearing?

That could also happen when I sat still, clipboard in hand, listening interiorly. But it seemed to happen less frequently.

Eventually I shifted over to journaling directly into my computer. It made sense; I was already copying the significant journal entries into it, anyway. I put what He said in italics, bold and blue. And since much of it was intensely personal, I put it all under password protection.

And under the most important protection: the shed Blood of Christ.

This needs to be said: This dialoguing process is only

for those who have had a personal encounter with Jesus Christ and have given their lives to Him. Why?

Because they know beyond the shadow of a doubt—in the depths of their hearts, as well as in their heads—that He *is* the living, risen Son of God. They know that at the name of Jesus, *every* knee shall bow. They know that He shed His Blood at Calvary to redeem each of us from our sins. By His Blood we are cleansed from all unrighteousness.

The name of Jesus and the power of His Blood—these are our weapons, all we need to do battle with principalities and powers. But we must *know* this at every level, with every particle of our being.

Early in my walk with the Lord, He allowed me to be tested by an angel of light and other principalities and powers because head knowledge alone would not be enough to do spiritual battle with the enemy. I had to *know* the power of the name of Jesus and the Blood of the Lamb. And the only way to know it absolutely, was to walk through it, using them to defeat the enemy.

It will be the same for you. If you pursue this listening process, sooner or later you will encounter a deceiving spirit, pretending to be Him. God allows this, because the only way to know for certain that you are hearing the right voice is to experience a wrong one.

A friend of mine, whom I had led into dialoguing with Him, later encountered such a spirit. It began to direct them. They became confused—and forgot that the author of confusion and the author of fear were one and the same. They became so hurt and distrustful that they stopped dialoguing entirely—until a year later when they attended another of my workshops, during which God encouraged them to resume their conversation.

So whenever I sit down to dialogue with Him, I first plead the Blood of Jesus over my mind, body, soul, and spirit. I can still be hearing self, instead of Him. But the Blood-covering makes it less likely I am hearing an unclean spirit pretending to be Him.

Regarding that possibility, the devil is more clever than you or I. He or one of his minions might slip in, undetected—especially if we are in a state of emotional turmoil, or if our ego has received a staggering blow.

For this reason, we are called by God's Word to test the spirits. And in the fourth chapter of John's first epistle, He provides the test. Stop and ask the voice, *"Let me hear you say, 'Jesus Christ is Lord, come in the flesh.'"* (see 1 John 4:2-4). An unclean spirit cannot utter those words, for to do so would be to admit that it was indeed defeated.

Yet even this test should not be regarded as infallible. If, for instance, your faith, without your being aware of it, has shifted from the name and the Blood, and into the testing ritual itself, it will not have the power it should have.

In the end, it boils down to our ability to know the voice—and the heart—of the Shepherd. Jesus explained our relationship to Him in the tenth chapter of the gospel of John. The Shepherd trains us to know His voice. He calls us by name and leads us out. (see John 10:3-10.) We sheep, who run away at the voice of a stranger, are to discern the spirit and intent of the one who is speaking to us. Is it a thief, coming to steal, kill, and destroy? Or is it Him, coming that we might have life, and have it to the full?

Sorting out the voice of the Shepherd from the voice of our own desire is more difficult. Particularly when what we desire is something God might also intend for us. Praying recently about a friend who had long believed a self-generated distortion in their journal, I heard, *When you want something to be true, enough to force it to be true in your own mind, then you hear the voice of your soul, and not of My spirit.*

At this point it should be stated that this is no form of self-hypnosis. At all times I am in full control of my faculties, eyes open, senses alert. At no time do I ever invite any spirit to enter me and write through me. Such practices are occult, to be shunned by any true believer.

You and I are Blood-bought children of the Lamb, in full possession of our minds, bodies, souls, and spirits at all times. We are merely recording words that come into our hearts. We can stop at any moment (and sometimes have to, when the baby cries or the phone rings).

The final test? Having pled the Blood and tested the spirit, examining its underlying motivation, compare what you have heard with Scripture. It must line up perfectly with the Word, both in letter and in spirit.

But no test is infallible. And no one is immune from being duped. Recently I was apprehensive about an impending meeting. Rebuking the author of fear (yet still caught in it), I went to my journal, which seemed to confirm that the thing I feared the most was about to come upon me.

I asked the voice to declare that Jesus Christ was Lord, come in the flesh. It did. So I went on listening, as it added reasons for being fearful that had not occurred to me. By the time of the meeting I was filled with dread.

But God had mercy. He put so much grace on me that not only could I feel it; I could almost *see* it, mounded up like white spun candy. I need fear no evil. He was with me—beside me, within me, around me. I could relax and listen with a heart filled with only love.

The next morning, when I asked Him how I could have been deceived by an angel of light after all these years, He showed me that I had neglected to test the spirit behind the spirit. The voice I had listened to was counseling a pre-emptive counter-attack. And I so loathed the spineless jellyfish I'd become that I believed I was hearing God, stiffening my backbone, preparing me for battle.

Had I properly weighed the spirit of what was being said, I would have seen it was not the voice of the Shepherd who has only love in His heart for His sheep —all of them.

   Moral? There are times when you *should* distrust your journal—let it go and leave it be for awhile. I should have. But because my heart was turned to God, He resolved the situation—wonderfully.

How often did I journal? As often as necessary. When the pressures of the day would mount unbearably, or when I would get blindsided by events I never saw coming, I would fly to my journal. I didn't always like what He told me, but invariably He calmed me down and let me see the situation from His perspective.

One time, after a bruising confrontation with my publishers, I grabbed up my clipboard and furiously wrote:

You were there, Father! You heard what they said! You know what they've done! You know how difficult they are to work with!

My son, have you any idea how difficult you *are to work with? How often they have come to Me about* you?

Funny how quickly the starch went out of my shirt.

One thing I could always count on from Him was dead-level honesty, which I tried to match, as there was little point to any of this if we didn't start there. I could accept His honesty, because it came from such a depth of understanding. He *was* compassion. He knew me utterly—the worst. Ugly things I didn't even suspect about myself. And *still* He loved me.

His love was beyond all human comprehension. And He'd been waiting all my life for me to realize it.

The perfect Father loved His far-from-perfect son. And now we were building a relationship.

As I mentioned, much of what we discussed lay in areas where both of us wanted to see me change. Unforgiveness, self-centeredness, ego, sloth, jealousy—nothing new. Nothing He had not been dealing with for years.

The difference was, now I *wanted* to change (or thought I did).

Four years ago we got to the bottom of my core sin—unforgiveness. I was on Bermuda to outline my third mystery, which would be set there to provide a change of venue from Cape Cod. My hero, a modern-day monk named Bartholomew, was at the edge of spiritual burnout. I sent him down there on an extended personal retreat.

When Brother Bart asked his superior how long his exile would last, he was told that if a date was set for his return, he would just stonewall it—do his time and come home, unchanged. (He and I were much alike.) He was down there to reconnect with God. Once he had, God would tell him when it was time to go home.

The publisher suggested I go and do likewise.

Been there, done that, I protested.

But I'd not gone as Brother Bartholomew.

There was no arguing with that. Unfortunately the

only time open was the week between Christmas and New Year's—the worst time to be anywhere but home.

I arrived in Bermuda with a major chip on my shoulder. I resented the publisher, Bermuda, the mystery series, God, you name it. I would stay in the Quarry Cottage, atop the hill on the Heydon Trust property in Somerset. Situated in an ancient, abandoned quarry, the nicest thing about it was its quaint name. It was a one-room, twelve-by-eighteen-foot cement cubicle—in an architectural style I dubbed Early Maginot Line.

Father Arthur Lane, the retired Episcopal priest who was director of the Trust then, met me at the airport. Leaving me at the cottage, he explained that the three sisters who helped him look after the place had stocked the refrigerator. If I needed anything else, the Piggly Wiggly, the local grocery store, was in Somerset, a half-hour walk down the old railway right-of-way. Other than at daily Mass, this would be the last I would see of him.

After two days of peanut-butter sandwiches, I found an excuse to go down to the big house: I needed to send a fax to the States. I could have done this at any time, but I elected to do it just before noon—well aware that lunch was their big meal of the day.

The sisters were in the kitchen. One was stirring a savory pot of stew. Another was tossing a fresh green salad. Another was removing a fresh-baked loaf of bread from the oven.

Seeing me, the stew sister smiled. "You're joining us for lunch, aren't you, David?"

"We have plenty," added the bread sister, cutting into the loaf and filling the kitchen with its heavenly aroma. "More than we can eat."

"I'll set another place," concluded the salad sister, opening the silverware drawer.

I was just thanking God for His servant Benedict who had urged his followers to put such an emphasis on hospitality—treat each visitor as if he were Jesus Himself—when Father Lane appeared at the kitchen door.

"David is not staying for lunch," he informed the sisters. "He's here on a personal retreat. He'll be eating by himself. Up there." He nodded in the direction of the Quarry Cottage.

Without a word, I left and trudged back up the hill—adding Father Lane to the top of the list of things I hated about Bermuda.

That afternoon, though there was still plenty to eat in the fridge, I walked to the grocery store, determined to have a feast that night, limited only by how much I could carry back.

I would have the best tossed salad ever—with diced turkey, baby carrots, Bermuda onion, minced garlic, feta cheese, all on a bed of baby spinach, drizzled with balsamic vinegar, and the most expensive olive oil in the Piggly Wiggly. On the side I would have toasted pita bread with aged Parmesan melted on it. And for dessert? Well, when in BDA, eat what the Bermudians loved— rum raisin ice cream!

In the store I'd soon filled my little cart. But as I reached for the pint of ice cream, I got a distinct check in my spirit.

No.

No? I'd not asked His input, much less invited Him along on this venture. In fact, I'd purposely excluded Him. I reached again for the ice cream.

What part of "no" do you not understand?

Normally I appreciated His wry humor. Not today.

"Why can't I have it?" I demanded aloud like a truant four-year-old, startling the lady next to me. I knew perfectly well why not: My cholesterol was 228.

Because I said so.

Glowering, I did not add the ice cream to the cart.

But on the way out, I fished a discarded newspaper out of the trash barrel by the door. On a personal retreat, one was supposed to eschew anything that would draw one back into the world—radio, television, cell phones, magazines, music. Newspapers.

Supper did not taste as good as I'd hoped—possibly because I'd made a point of *not* asking His blessing beforehand, let alone inviting Him to join me. (At that moment, I was in anti-Benedictine mode.)

Leaving the dirty dishes in the sink, I read the *Mid-Ocean News* from cover to cover. Unfortunately that edition was only twelve pages, so it wasn't long before I was reading about a cricket match in Sri Lanka. And I loathed cricket.

After I'd read every word, I went to bed. At 8:00—which was early, even for me.

Turning out the light, I made a point of not saying goodnight to God.

7

As We Forgive

Three hours later I woke up, covered with goose bumps—the bad kind. There was someone in the cottage with me. I looked around. Though it was dark, there was enough moonlight coming in to see there was no one there. No one visible.

What I was sensing, I realized, was a presence—an evil presence. A large, imposing one.

Bermuda was an island of stark contrasts. It had witchcraft and Caribbean voodoo. It also had more churches per capita than any place on earth. This meant that extreme light and extreme darkness could often be found side by side.

Shuddering, I pled the Blood of Jesus over my mind, body, soul, and spirit. That definitely helped. It banished my fear.

But it did not banish the presence—whatever it was.

Now what?

Ask for a warrior angel.

I did not acknowledge that thought as coming from God, because as far as I was concerned, He and I were no longer on speaking terms. But it seemed like a pretty good idea—something I'd never heard of.

All right, Father, send down a warrior angel. A big one.

Instantly the presence disappeared.

Relieved and grateful, I still wasn't sure I wanted to talk to Him.

Is this the way friends treat friends?

Who says we're friends?

I do.

Well, if this is the way *You* treat Your friends, it's no wonder You have so few of them!

It hurt when Thérèse said that, and it hurts when you say it.

Good! Now You know what it feels like!

I know.

Sleep was now out of the question. And since He seemed determined to talk, I picked up my clipboard—which I'd not touched since I packed to come down.

All right, Father, I wrote, what do You want of me?

You can stop behaving like a child.

That stung—because I was, I realized, having a

temper tantrum. And like a child stuck in one, I didn't seem able to get out of it on my own. So I was grateful He'd called me on it—sort of.

Forgive me, Father, for I have sinned.

Don't be flippant.

Sorry.

And give up your self-pity; it's only anger, denied an external focus.

You're quoting a Salada teabag.

They were quoting Me.

What am I angry about?

What do you think?

He was doing the Zen thing again. In the beginning, when we first started dialoguing, He would patiently answer every question I put to Him. In fact, I used it as a way to reconnect, if I ever hit a dry spell.

But increasingly, as I grew accustomed to hearing His voice and talking with Him, when I would ask Him a question, He would ask it back to me, as a Zen master might respond to a questioning pupil. He wanted me to make the spiritual effort involved in arriving at the answer. We both knew I was lazy, that my spiritual muscles were flabby. By making me do the work, instead of doing it for me, He was building them up.

All right, I wrote, I'm angry at being down here in

Bermuda, and being totally out of control. I'm angry at You, Father, because You arranged this.

Who else are you angry at?

Father Lane.

My son, he was only doing what I bade him do.

I see that. It must have cost him.

It usually does. It was especially difficult for him, because he is fond of you.

Well, you know what? Now—I love him!

Good. He is my gift to you.

We're still working through the thing with my earthly father, aren't we.

Yes.

But that's not the reason we're talking, is it? I mean, other than getting on speaking terms again.

You mean, you giving up your pique.

Sorry, Father. And I mean it.

I know you do. Forgiven. In fact, forgiveness is what I want to talk to you about. There are six people you have not forgiven.

We'd reached the heart of it, I sensed—the reason He'd brought me down here.

I knew the six he meant. But I *had* forgiven them, I insisted. It had been a matter of life and death that I do so. Literally. Unforgiveness was what had opened the door to the cancer, and I had come perilously close to dying.

It was a big problem with me. If someone intentionally wronged me, I didn't just get back; I got even. And I could wait a long time, if necessary—as long as it took. Whoever said revenge was a dish best supped cold, knew what they were talking about.

At the very least, if it was someone with whom I could not avoid frequent contact, I would turn off the faucet on their personality, as if they had ceased to exist.

But after nearly dying of cancer, I had sought to make amends. I had gone to each one and forgiven them—and asked them to forgive me for holding them in unforgiveness. I had said and done all the things a good Christian was supposed to.

And You *know* that, I added emphatically to God, hurt that He would think otherwise.

Have you truly forgiven them?

You mean, I haven't? (Obviously He meant that, dummy!)

What do you think?

If I truly had, He wouldn't be Zenning me again, so—I thought about it. After a while I admitted: Well, I do occasionally fantasize about one or another of them.

What sort of fantasy?

He knew. He just wanted me to hear it out of my own mouth. So I described it.

Occasionally (I did not do this often) I fantasize about them standing before You on their day of judgment. You and they review the movie of their life. You have the remote, and each time they do something—intentionally or unintentionally—that hurts someone else, you press the pause button, freezing the action, so they can absorb the full impact and ramifications of what they did and why, and the ripple effect it had on other lives. Pause, pause, pause, pause, pause—until they are so revulsed at who they are at the core of their very being, they start vomiting uncontrollably!

I looked down at what I had just written and added: That doesn't sound very much like forgiveness.

No, it doesn't.

What do You want me to do?

Forgive them.

I thought I had. What do I need to do?

Pray for each one of them, every day, for the rest of their life, or yours, whichever ends first.

I can do that, I wrote quickly—a little too quickly.

I don't want a rattled-off prayer. I want you to see each one's face as you pray for them. And I want you to believe that as you pray for them, I am blessing them.

I knew He was aware of the resistance level rising in my heart. Why am I resisting this? I asked.

Why do you think?

So I thought about it, and wrote: I guess, because if You do bless them, and their day momentarily brightens, they don't deserve it.

I shook my head and added: And that doesn't sound much like forgiveness, either.

No, it doesn't. But if you will do this, My son, you will be more blessed than they. And you need no longer fear your six-month checkups.

He got me there. Anyone who ever had cancer removed had to go back every six months for an x-ray and a CAT scan to make sure it had not returned. Two days before each checkup I would start getting depressed, till, by the time we arrived at Mass General, I was positively morbid. And then giddy with joy when I was given a reprieve. And it was as hard on Barbara as it was on me.

All right, I wrote. I'll do it.

And I have—with amazing results! Two I now love like kin—actually, better than kin. Two I now really like. And two have moved from dark to neutral.

There was nothing new in this. Any time you prayed consistently for someone, your relationship with that person was bound to improve. And like Job, you would be blessed in the process. Job's ordeal ended, the moment he prayed for his friends. (See Job 42:10.) But it was new to me.

I yawned. It had been a wonderful evening; one of our best. But it was now long past midnight, and I was ready for bed.

We're not done.

What do You mean?

What about all the people you have hurt?

Me?

You.

Have I not asked them to forgive me?

Most of them. I'm referring to the ones you hurt before you knew Me.

Father, is this trip really necessary? I mean, isn't there some dispensation for not knowing we'd be held accountable?

Pause, pause, pause…

All right, all right! But that was a long time ago. I don't think I can remember…

I will refresh your memory.

And He did—for four more hours. I asked His forgiveness for each incident He showed me. And got sicker and sicker of who I was, at the core of my very being. I did not start vomiting uncontrollably, but I felt like it. I'd had a bellyful of me.

Father, I wrote, as the sky outside began to brighten, I do not like who I am; in fact, I detest me.

Good. I want you to remember who you are in your unredeemed nature, any time you are tempted to think more highly of yourself than you ought, or to hold someone else in unforgiveness.

8

Short-Roping

You would think that having unlimited access to God—to talk things over with Him as a friend, whenever you felt like it for as long as you liked—would be the most wonderful thing in a person's life. You would think it would rank right up there, after discovering He was real, and that He cared. You would think it would change a person's life, radically and permanently.

It should.

It didn't.

Listening to Him was, after all, just another form of prayer. And as mentioned, prayer was a notoriously easy habit to break. In time, my conversations with God became perfunctory.

I would start the day off with Him, because whenever I did, things went better. And whenever I didn't, they had a way of deteriorating at a precipitous pace.

But I would set the agenda. I would decide when we would talk, and when we were finished. I would bring up the topics we would cover, and which we would leave alone. (There were increasingly large areas of my life that were not open to discussion.)

Some days were simply too busy to begin with half an hour of quiet time with Him. I would hit the deck running. He knew my schedule; He would understand.

When I thought about it, I *was* vaguely concerned about what was happening to my prayer life. I sensed that my relationship with Him got either better or worse; it never stayed the same.

We were drifting apart—to the point where He had to resort to dreams to get my attention on certain things. Interpreting them was never hard; He showed me their meaning the moment I asked Him. They usually involved something I had done that needed repenting of.

My heart was still towards Him—but a little less so, week by week. I didn't know what to do about it, and it was fast getting to the point where even if I *did* know, I might not choose to.

He knew what to do about it. He took matters into His own hands.

Paraclete Press had decided to start a mystery series, with a modern-day monk as its protagonist. Was I interested?

I jumped at the chance. All my life I'd wanted to work in fiction. But at this late stage in my career, I could not afford to invest two years in a novel—one to write it, another to line up a publisher—with the chance that no one might want it. This way, if it was halfway decent, it would see the light of day. I signed a three-book contract.

To get the first one under way, I stayed with friends in Phoenix for a month. My lighthouse office at home was a writer's dream—but I lived in a residential Christian community with three hundred and fifteen very active members. It was like being on an aircraft carrier in a battle zone. Visitors invariably commented on the peace they experienced on the flight deck—without realizing it was there, because below deck every crew member was doing exactly what they were called to do, every minute.

The hum level at home mitigated against the gathering of gossamer—figments of ideas before they solidified—the first stage of any fiction project.

My first week in Arizona I spent flame-dancing — circling the fire, dipping in, finding it too hot, and ducking back out again. In my case, the dance consisted of sketching suspects and protagonists, scenes and dialogue—"getting to know my characters," I called it.

Inevitably the morning came when I could no longer put off the actual start. I stared down at the blank legal pad on my lap and faced the truth: I did not know the first thing about writing a mystery. The sum total of my experience amounted to watching a few installments of *Murder She Wrote* I vaguely knew that you had a murder, added potential suspects to the pot, and continued to stir as it came to a boil, until the amateur sleuth figured out whodunit—one page ahead of the reader.

But that was all I knew. And it was too late to run to Barnes and Noble to get something off the "How to Write a Mystery" shelf. It was too late to do anything, except pray.

Father, I wrote in white panic, I feel like I'm standing at the edge of a precipice, and my foot has just slipped. I've lost my balance and am falling into the abyss. Unless You reach out right now and save me, I'm doomed.

Organize your elements.

"I don't even know what my elements *are!*" I cried aloud.

Silence.

I wondered if He'd heard me—if He even cared. And then, in rapid-fire succession, came elements.

Tighten the suspense.
Arrest the wrong suspect.
Throw suspicion in a different direction.
Have a second murder.

I jotted them down as fast as they came, and after an hour or so, there were one hundred and thirty seven. I was trembling. I'd just experienced a miracle, on a par with getting my missing shirt back in answer to my first prayer.

God had done what I'd begged Him to do. He'd reached out and saved me. But I still didn't know what to do.

Organize your elements.

I was dying to ask Him how—but I knew He'd just turn it back to me. So I stared at the three pages of elements—and realized what I needed to do.

I got some yellow Post-it notes, and on each put an element. Soon, the glass doors of a breakfront cabinet were decorated with a blizzard of yellow Post-it notes.

Praying much, I decided which one came first, and put it at the top of the door seam down the middle of the cabinet. Then deciding which came next, I put it under the first one. Each took a good deal of thought, and I often changed my mind, grateful for the re-stickability of Post-it notes.

After three days, they resembled the last Christmas tree on the lot—spiky on top, bulbous on the bottom. After three more days, they were in a straight line. It was another goose-bumps moment: I was looking at the plotline—the outline for the outline.

He didn't have to tell me what to do next. As editor of Doubleday Canada, I'd watched Lee Barker in our New York office working with Canadian author Arthur Hailey as they developed *Airport*. The first outline was a sentence per chapter. The second outline was a paragraph per chapter. The third outline was a page per chapter. Then let the writing commence.

Heretofore, writing history or ghostwriting other people's stories, the foundation was already there in the chronology of events. All I had to do was decide where to put the emphasis. With fiction, however, there was no foundation; you were creating out of thin air.

By the time I finished my third outline (my foundation), it was fourteen thousand words long—for a book that was meant to be no more than eighty thousand. Which I now *knew* I could write.

As it turned out, the outline—figuring out how each scene was going to lead into the next, and keeping all the subplots progressing at the same pace—was the heavy lifting. I was not used to sustaining concentration at this level of intensity, like a chess master narrowing the world down to sixty-four squares. I was tired frequently and I took lots of little naps.

In the evenings I was reading *The Climb*, Anatoli Bookreev's account of the tragedy on Mount Everest. The only man to summit Everest without bottled oxygen, Bookreev vividly described climbing above eight thousand meters. One took a step and then had to rest half a minute, to gather the energy to take the next step.

It sounded like what I was doing, I told God, as I emerged from one of my energy-gathering naps.

Don't worry, My son; I'm short-roping you.

He was referring to the unpublicized practice of strong guides hauling weak but wealthy clients to the summit. I was grateful—sort of.

Actually, I was jealous—of how much help He was giving me. I know how ridiculous that sounds, but it's the truth. And one morning I confronted Him with it.

Father, You know what this reminds me of? Christmas morning, when I was nine.

My big present that year had been an Erector set. As soon as I'd unwrapped it, my father announced that he and I were going to attempt the most difficult project in the instruction manual—a working model of a windmill. So, right there next to the Christmas tree, we began. It wasn't long before I noticed he was giving me the simple pieces to assemble. All the really tricky stuff, he was doing himself.

I could almost hear God chuckle as He replied, *Don't worry, My son; only a few discerning readers will know how much I helped you. The rest will assume you did it all yourself.*

Once we'd finished the last outline, the actual writing was a breeze. In fact, it was fun—something I'd never said about writing. I woke up one morning and could hardly wait to get to the computer, to see what my characters were going to say and do next.

With a shock I realized I'd become a *writer*. Up to that moment I was just someone who wrote books; it's what I did. And I used to resent other wordsmiths who rhapsodized to Charlie Rose or Brian Lamb about the thrill of being writers. Now I knew it, too.

And I knew whom to thank—the One I'd only invited into my so-called area of expertise at the threat of plummeting into the abyss. The One who enjoyed creating with me, as much as I enjoyed creating with Him. Who loved participating with anyone who created, because He *was* the Creator. Of everything.

9

The Expansion

Writing mysteries was as far out of my professional comfort zone as it was possible to get—as God knew it would be. It forced me to lean upon Him, and the more I did, the more dependent I became upon His input.

He would never do it *for* me. He always made me do the actual work. But He never hesitated to let me know what He thought of what I was doing.

He was a tough editor in the best sense, teaching me that the number-one enemy of *'best'* was *'good'*. He was like the teacher you sought out at a high-school reunion, the one who would never let you settle for less than the best you were capable of.

As I wrote, I could sense Him behind me, looking over my shoulder as the words appeared on the monitor. He called me to be ever more discriminating, reminding me of what Alistair Cooke learned as a young man at Oxford.

"Cooke," declared one of his dons, "you must learn to murder your darlings!" In other words, that phrase or point you adored, might have to wind up on the cutting-room floor.

My editor and writing partner was a little more compassionate than that don—but only a little.

Needless to say, I was now striving to please Him. And as in any good student/teacher relationship, I desired to spend as much time with Him as possible. What a difference from the pre-mystery days!

To finish the second mystery, I went down to Bermuda for a month. Each morning we would talk, before I started work. And because talking with Him was more enjoyable than working, the dialogue sessions got longer and longer.

One morning, after a couple of hours talking over this and that, I said, You know, Father, I could go on all day like this!

I'm enjoying it, too, my son. But a little less Mary, a little more Martha.

After that, whenever it was time for me to get down to work, it was Martha-time.

Each morning we would start off with an assessment of the day before. My son, I am pleased with you. Or, My son, I am displeased with you. Occasionally, when I was stubborn, He would tell me He was vexed with me. And once He said He was disgusted with me (which made two of us).

Regarding His calling me "My son," a friend who'd been recording his conversations with God years before I began, wondered if that might not be my self, wanting to hear Him call me that.

It might be, I admitted. Or it might be that the Father knew how badly I'd longed for the approval of my earthly father, which I'd never received.

In any event, as the second mystery was drawing to a close, one morning He started our session with a startling pronouncement: *My son, today you have more than pleased me. You have delighted My heart. Ask me anything right now, and I will grant it.*

Whoa! Did I hear Him right? He repeated it.

I was stunned. I felt like I was in a Grimm's fairytale, and had just been given one wish. All I could think was, *Don't blow it!*

What should I ask for? Money? Long life?

The thing was, I felt so close to Him now, none of

those things mattered. If He gave me money, I would use it for serving Him. As for long life, if He wanted to take me home now, fine. If He wanted me to serve Him another twenty years, fine.

I could ask for wisdom like Solomon did. That worked pretty well in the beginning—until he got bored.

Um, let me get back to you, I wrote, putting Him on hold, as it were.

I went out for a long walk. When I returned, I wrote: All right, I've figured out what I want. When I first met you, you called me to write for you. I left Doubleday to do that. Then you called me to live in a Christian community. I left Princeton to do that. Now I'm asking you to expand my call further. I want to encourage other old hands who've known you a long time, that they can regain their first love of you. Because that is what has happened to me.

You have chosen wisely, my son. I grant your request.

The expansion began as soon as I got home. One by one, He would bring old hands to me—wounded, in despair, scarcely believing that He cared about them any more.

Before meeting with each one, I would ask Him for input and discernment. He would tell me what tack to take and what tone. Sometimes He would give me a word of wisdom or knowledge that would trigger a lost memory or unlock a closet in the heart. With each, He would give me the grace to convince them that He *did* care, and that they *could* hear Him in the depths of their heart.

Three months later, the process got a significant boost. Our community was hosting an experimental writers' workshop. Asked to round up the usual suspects, I called the resident poets, scriptwriters, and short-story writers.

You come, too, I was told.

I tried to beg off. I led writers' workshops myself, each summer at Gordon Conwell Seminary. For me, it would be a busman's holiday.

But when I asked God if He wanted me there, He did. Why? He wouldn't tell me. All He would say was that by the end of the workshop, I would know.

The leader ran a good workshop. As I did in mine, she made extensive use of flash-writing exercises. These were similar to improvisational theater workshop assignments. The leader would give the writers a one-, two-, or three-character situation, then have them begin a very short story based on the scene that had just been set for them. As in improv work, they were to free-write—composing from the heart, not the head. Writing intuitively, whatever came.

The purpose of such an exercise was to free their writing from the shackles of intellectual constraint. Too many beginning writers were paralyzed or severely hobbled by what the practical side of their nature was dictating. Their creative instincts were being stifled or shut down entirely by their internal editor.

Flash-writing exercises were useful, if only to limber up their imagination and show them how many different ways there were up the mountain.

At the end of the workshop, she gave us a final flash-writing exercise—that blew me away. It was a two-character setting that put the writer in direct dialogue with Jesus—exactly what I'd been doing every morning for six years.

10

Connecting

There are more than four thousand instances in Scripture of God walking with man, talking to man, communing with man. Many of the psalms are David's side (and sometimes God's) of his ongoing dialogue with his Creator.

Yet most of His children today do not believe they can actually hear Him in the depths of their being, let alone carry on a conversation with Him. Instead, they believe the lie that even though the Spirit of God indwells them, they cannot hear His still, small voice within. If they do hear Him, they dismiss it as their own imagined thoughts.

The leader's final exercise, I saw, would get anyone who loved God and wanted to live for Him, over the final, largely imaginary roadblock that kept them from communicating directly with Him.

The only trouble was, it was hers. She had developed it and would soon be using it in workshops. If I was ever to use such a technique to connect others in dialogue with God, I would have to develop my own method.

When I asked God how, He suggested I recast it as an interactive short story, set in Jerusalem nineteen centuries ago. It would still be a flash-writing exercise, leading one into dialogue with Jesus, but that would be the only similarity in our techniques.

As it happened, Gordon Conwell's week-long writers' workshop was starting in another week. I asked God if He would have me introduce the exercise there. He would. But I was still apprehensive—what would the reaction be?

I waited until the last session of the last day. By that time the eight people in the popular fiction track (mine) had forged a bond of trust. They had become comfortable critiquing each other's work, with me showing them the balance between encouragement and useful editorial correction.

"Before we break up," I announced, "I have one more flash-writing exercise for you. This one's a little different. Instead of having three minutes to think about how you're going to do it, you're to start writing the moment I finish setting the scene. And instead of taking five minutes, you can have fifteen."

I set the scene, started them off, and left the room.

When I returned, five were still writing. Of these, three were in tears as they wrote.

I asked them if any of them would like to share what they'd written. Normally this would be required. Part of becoming a professional was being able to submit your work to colleagues, without apologizing for it beforehand. But in this case it might be intensely personal, so I left the sharing optional.

Nevertheless, by now we were friends—and friends trusted friends. One by one, they shared their dialogues with Jesus. There was no question that seven of the eight had connected with Him. The eighth knew Jesus was in Heaven, so instead of doing the assignment, she described Heaven as she imagined it.

In the days following the workshop, I got e-mails from three of the group. They had continued the dialoguing process at home—and it had transformed their lives.

The next group I tried it on was Pen—our writers' group in the community. All nine connected.

When people outside the community heard what I was doing, other groups asked me to lead them in the exercise, too. And most connected.

The acid test came when a retired pastor, hungry for a more intimate relationship with God, asked if he could borrow the exercise overnight. I hesitated; always before, I'd been there to put it over, answer questions, make sure it went the way it was supposed to. Now, I would see if the bird was ready to leave the nest. Would it fly on its own?

In the morning, the pastor returned, ecstatic. "This is the best thing that's happened to me since I first came to the Lord!"

For me, the best thing was that the exercise flew, unassisted. It didn't need a workshop setting. It didn't need me. It would work anywhere, under any circumstances.

One thing I stressed from the outset: This was *only* for those who already had a praying relationship with God. I stopped short of limiting it to Christians, because Jews had been walking and talking with God long before He gave us His only begotten Son. (Tevye was only the most recent example.)

But it did seem to work best for those who understood the power of the shed Blood of Christ. And those already comfortable with the presence of the Holy Spirit seemed to have the easiest time of it.

I soon realized there were other caveats I needed to stress when leading anyone in the exercise, aside from the test in First John 4. It was always a good idea to periodically check your journal with someone in whose discernment you had confidence. Especially when your journaling involved something you very much desired. With the exception of the Bible, received prophetic words were always suspect—because they came through an imperfect filter (you and me). None of us was so free of self that we could be certain the words we received were untainted.

Friends have pointed out to me where my ego insinuated itself into my journal—even in places where I was sure it was pure God. Recently, in fact, He rebuked me for attempting to put words of encouragement in His mouth. *There will be times when I encourage you, My son. But it will be when I choose to, not when you want Me to.*

So now, whenever He says anything encouraging, I always ask Him to say: "Jesus Christ is Lord, come in the flesh." He doesn't mind.

Conversely, I warn people who have just connected with God, that they will soon hear, if they haven't already, a voice say, *That's not Him talking to you. That's nothing but wish fulfillment, what you imagine He might say to you, if He were ever to talk to the likes of you.*

If they are Charismatic, I tell them it's the same voice who told them when they first started praying in an unknown tongue, *That's not a prayer language! That's nothing but gibberish! Self-generated babel!*

The antidote to such poison is the same now as it was then: Persevere. Ignore that voice. Write down what you receive, put a date in the margin, and look at it a day later. Then decide if you were hearing God. Or show it to a wise friend and let them discern it.

Too often we decide we can't hear God—because, in reality, we may not want to. Think what it means if we *can* hear Him. Conversion of the soul takes a great leap forward.

Some regard conversion as that moment when we confess to the Lord that we are sinners, ask Him to forgive our sins, and invite Him into our hearts to rule and reign there, as our Master, as well as our Savior. At that moment, we are born again. But it's not the end; it's only the beginning.

The rest of our lives are to be spent cooperating with the Holy Spirit, as He seeks to conform us ever more to the image of the Son. This lifelong process is the conversion of the soul. In other ages it was called the Way of the Cross, or the quest for holiness, or sanctification. A blessed few get the job done before they die; the rest of us spend the remainder of our allotted time working at it.

But if we can actually *hear* God, imagine how that would speed up the process! Instant accountability. Instant conviction and repentance. Life-giving insights, life-freeing truth—from the most gifted and loving Counselor there ever was!

Alas, conversion of the soul is often regarded as a threatening prospect. For conversion means change—sometimes, radical change. He might ask you to stop doing something (about which you may have already sensed His displeasure). Or He might ask you to start doing something you've been putting off. Either way, if you hear Him and commit it to paper, and then choose to disregard Him, you're in rebellion.

And so, many who are perfectly capable of hearing Him, prefer to believe they can't. Or if they can, they prefer not to write it down. Because once it's there in black and white, immutable, it holds two people accountable: you and Him.

A further reason to write it down is how quickly good seeds are snatched away, when we attempt to hold them in memory. Think back to the last time you had a vivid dream and thought you really needed to write it down. But by the time you finished brushing your teeth, most or all of it was gone.

When you do the exercise in the next chapter, keep in mind, God can see into your heart and your mind. He already knows how you feel and what you are going to say. The great *unknown* is how He will respond. Because no matter how certain you are of what He will say to you, He will invariably surprise you—if only by the depth of His love for you.

So keep your side of the dialogue short. There will be times in the future when you'll feel compelled to pour it all out anyway. He understands the need for venting. But for now, don't tell Him what He already knows. *Listen.*

Regarding the depth of His love, do not be surprised if the first thing you hear Him tell you is how much He loves you. In some cases, He repeats it over and over. (A friend of mine heard only "I love you" for six months.) The reason for this is that so many of us privately consider ourselves unlovable, even by Him.

As in any new relationship, the first thing that should happen is the establishment of a bond of trust. Love, flowing both ways, is how that happens. If you'll open your heart to Him, you'll soon be dumbfounded by the magnitude of His love. He can speak the strongest truth—the very thing that might have devastated you when spoken by a well-meaning friend—and from Him you'll be able to hear it because of the infinite compassion and understanding with which it comes. It won't be what He says; it will be the way He says it.

The day will quickly come when you'll be so awed by His transcending, transfiguring love, you'll reread what Paul wrote about love to the believers in Corinth (1 Corinthians 13). And you will weep—for joy.

Trust takes time. You can't hurry it. It took me five years to finally trust Him to the depth and core of my being—to the point where, no matter what happened, I would never doubt His love for me. It has taken another four years for me to demonstrate that He can begin to trust me.

Trust is what must happen if any relationship is to go forward. And trust is founded on love.

Finally, the exercise in the next chapter is only a means to an end. There's no magic in it. Its sole function is to connect you with God. Once you've made the connection, you can forget about the exercise. You'll be able to reconnect with Him anytime, anywhere, under any circumstances.

Just spread the wings of your spirit and soar!

11

The Olive Grove

(This chapter will set the scene for a flash-writing exercise with two voices. Have pen and paper handy, and at the end, start writing the dialogue. From the heart. Whatever comes, go with it, and take as long as you like.)

Y ou're in Jerusalem, nineteen centuries ago. You've come for the high holy days, and this year it seems every Jew in Israel has had the same idea. Every bed, every corner, has been taken.

You let your family talk you into coming. Not that it took much persuading; you heard the Galilean would be there—the Master everyone's talking about. Judea, Galilee, Samaria, even Gadara—wherever He's been, there've been miracles. Healing miracles—of mind, soul, and spirit, as well as of the body.

You could use healing—in all four realms. So you

came. And dared hope that somehow, despite the crowds around Him, you might find a private moment with Him. That's all it would take. You've heard about the woman healed by touching the hem of His garment, the blind man whose sight was restored, the servant and the little girl raised from the dead. And you know in your heart it's true—*all* of it.

But it's hopeless. The moment they hear where He is, everyone runs there.

So this morning you wander the dusty, sun-baked streets, wishing you were home—under the shade tree, with a cup of cool water by your side.

You enter a square, where the only shade is over there, under that blue awning of that vendor's cart. He's selling something to drink—water, flavored with a little honey.

Parched, you go over. There's only one person ahead of you—a young man, sandy-haired, quick smile under a perpetual frown. With a water yoke he's brought two jars, which the old vendor is filling for him, ladling from a massive urn.

Finishing, the old man asks, "Will He—be teaching this evening?"

"He may be."

"Don't you know? You're one of the ones with Him."

The young man smiles. "We never know—where we're going or when. We're learning it doesn't matter, as long as we're with Him."

"Living that way—isn't it hard?"

"It *is!*" exclaims the young man, laughing. "And I'm the worst at it! I *never* think things are going to work out! And they *always* do!"

As the vendor adjusts the jars under the yoke, the young man pulls out a coin purse.

The vendor holds up a hand. "It's a gift."

"It's too much! Let me pay."

The older man just smiles and shakes his head.

The young man looks at him. "Come to the Temple steps tomorrow morning," he says softly. "Before dawn. I can't promise, but the last two mornings He's been there at first light." And shouldering the yoke, he departs.

The vendor turns to you, eyebrows raised. But you shake your head and hurry after the young man— compelled by a thirst no honey-water can slake.

"Excuse me," you say, when you've caught up with him. "You're, um, one of His followers?"

He nods.

"Well—" For once, words fail you.

The young man stops and lowers the jars to the ground, lifting off the yoke and looking at you. "You want to meet Him?"

You nod.

"Alone?"

You nod emphatically.

He gazes into your eyes. And smiles. "You know the old olive grove on top of the mountain across the valley?"

"I've heard of it. Above the garden, isn't it?"

"That's the one. There's a path up to it, from the big cracked boulder at the south end of the valley. Start up it at noon."

You nod, and he sizes you up. "It's steep in places. And long—it'll take longer than you think." No smile now. "Can you do it?"

"I walked here, didn't I?" you snap. "It took us three days!" Then, more hesitantly, you add, "I think I can."

The young man's smile returns. "Use the climb as preparation."

"What do you mean?"

"You want to come to Him empty. Your mind clear, your heart free."

"How do I do that?"

"As you climb, ask God to help you set aside your cares and concerns, your feelings and emotions."

Straightening under the yoke, he raises the jars off the ground. You sense he's going there now. You could go with him!

But as if he knows what you're thinking, he smiles and says, "Noon. Come alone."

At noon you start up the path. It *is* steep. And rocky—he hadn't mentioned that. You've had to stop twice to get stones out of your sandals.

After climbing for half an hour or so, you come to an open place and wearily sit down on an old, bent-over cedar. Your feet are sore. Your back aches. Your lungs are burning. And he was right about one thing; it *is* longer than you thought—a *lot* longer.

Maybe this wasn't such a good idea. Maybe you should go back down. Now. No need to tell anyone. A fool's errand, that's all this was. Go down now, before you're missed.

A gentle breeze bearing the scent of oregano and rosemary caresses your cheek. You smile. This is not such a bad day. Gazing down at the Kidron Valley far below, stretching away into the hazy distance, you're surprised at how far you've come.

You remember the water skin slung from your shoulder. Carefully you remove its stopper and drink deeply. Not too much—you don't know how far it is to the top.

Then, taking a deep breath, you exhale and get to your feet. You can do this.

And suddenly you're glad to be on the mountain.

Only then do you notice the tree you've been sitting on. An icestorm must have bent it to that shape ages ago. It should have died—yet each spring it pushes out fresh green needles at the ends of its gnarled limbs.

Smiling, you resume your ascent. What was it that young man said about preparation? Ask God to help you set aside your cares and concerns.

Well, there are plenty of them! Will there be enough room for all of us tonight? Are we spending too much money? And what about everything I have to do when I get home?

One by one, you add each worry to an imaginary bag —and give it to Him. All right, God, You can have them—for now.

What was the other thing? Oh, yes, I'm supposed to

do the same with my feelings and emotions.

I've got plenty of *those!* Just the ones on this trip would fill a bundle!

Reflecting on them—and others—you add them to a second bag.

God, I give *them* to You, too!

You pause. Is there—anything else?

The old hurts. The unforgiveness.

You know what He's referring to.

I'm not sure I'm ready to give *those* to You. Not permanently. Not yet. But—maybe till I come down.

At last the path levels off. And there's the olive grove, just ahead. As you follow the path into its welcome shade, you smile. Your mind *is* clear, and your heart free.

In the grove, under the ancient olive trees, it's cooler. And it's still—not even insect sounds.

After all that sun, your eyes need a moment to adjust to the interplay of shifting shadows. When they do, you see that you are not alone. Over there, on the other side of the grove, next to what appears to be the ruins of an olive press, there's a man kneeling—a tall man, long hair, robed, head bowed.

The Galilean.

But now that you're *here*—and He's here—you feel funny about disturbing Him. He's praying.

Maybe this wasn't such a good idea. Maybe you should turn around now, and slip away…

Wait—He's raising His head. Looking at you. He smiles—and beckons you to come over.

Go ahead.

Yet—you hesitate.

He nods, still smiling. He means it.

You start towards Him.

He gets up now, and sits on a low stone ledge. And pats the wall next to Him. He wants you to join Him.

So—you do.

You sit down beside Him, and look into His eyes. And the two of you start to talk.

Now—without thinking about it or pre-editing it, write down what He says, what you say. Do it intuitively, from the heart, not the head. Whatever comes.

12

Once Upon a Prayer

As I began leading workshops for those interested in developing a dialogue with God, one thing troubled me. While anyone who had a heart for God could connect, not all pursued it.

They might be thrilled to discover they could indeed carry on a conversation with Him, and that He was interested in every aspect of their lives, with endless patience and perfect love. But when I would later ask them how it was going, they would often admit they'd not been in a listening mode for a while. Sometimes quite a while.

Of course, I went to Him about it.

My son, all I have called you to do is connect them with Me. What happens after that, is between them and Me. It is not your concern. Just keep out in front of Me, connecting them.

But…

I have called you to be a sower, not a harvester.

Why can't I be both?

You have neither the patience nor the compassion to be a harvester.

But…

Do not question Me, My son. Be grateful for the assignment I have given you. You will soon have all you can do, just to keep up with what I put before you. You are going to be My Johnny Appleseed for prayer.

Not long after that, I had a dream. In it, I was at the checkout counter of a bookstore, where there was a counter display of little books. It had a title I'd never heard of: *Once Upon a Prayer.*

When I woke up, my first thought was, *What a good title!* Then the significance of it struck me.

For some time I'd been thinking of distilling my Hearing-His-Voice workshop into a book. Through this dream, God seemed to be telling me it was time.

And since the adventure had begun in a popular fiction workshop for writers who had come to learn more about "once upon a time" and left having also learned more about prayer—what more fitting title?

One day, musing about where all this was leading, I asked Him about it.

This path You've put me on—it leads to surrender, doesn't it.

It does.

It's what used to be called "the Way of the Cross."

It is—a path well trodden, but few are on it today.

Well, as the pilgrims on the Camino might say, *Vaya con Dios.*

Vaya con Dios, My son.